EARTH'S ROCKY PAST

CRYSTALS

Richard Spilsbury

PowerKiDS
press™

New York

Published in 2016 by **The Rosen Publishing Group**
29 East 21st Street, New York, NY 10010

Produced for Rosen by Calcium

Editors for Calcium: Sarah Eason and Harriet McGregor
Designers: Paul Myerscough and Jessica Moon
Illustrator: Venetia Dean

Picture credits: Cover: Shutterstock: LVV; Inside: Dreamstime: Uldis Bindris 4b, Cornelius20 20r,
Dinozzaver 8r, Zsolt Bota Finna 21, Ekaterina Fribus 5b, Gavinp101 18–19, Hotshotsworldwide
17t, Gnel Karapetyan 7b, Ingemar Magnusson 14l, 22b, Carlos Soler Martinez 13t, Milahelp
SRO 13b, Tatiana Morozova 14r, 15l, Peter Sobolev 25r, Jennifer Thompson 9c, Vicente Barcelo
Varona 19t, Edward Westmacott 16, Simon Zenger 12; Shutterstock: Aarrows 20c, Baloncici
24–25, Fotana 27t, Jorg Hackemann 27b, Imfoto 23, 24t, Gil. K 26r, Lukiyanova Natalia/Frenta
6t, David Reilly 10–11, MarcelClemens 15r, J. Palys 22t, Albert Russ 1, 4t, Siim Sepp 6b, T.W. van
Urk 9b, Kozoriz Yuriy 11.

Cataloging-in-Publication Data
Spilsbury, Richard.
Crystals / by Richard Spilsbury.
p. cm. — (Earth's rocky past)
Includes index.
ISBN 978-1-4994-0833-1 (pbk.)
ISBN 978-1-4994-0832-4 (6 pack)
ISBN 978-1-4994-0831-7 (library binding)
1. Crystals — Juvenile literature. 2. Crystal growth — Juvenile literature.
3. Rocks — Analysis — Juvenile literature. I. Spilsbury, Richard, 1963-. II. Title.
QD921.S65 2016
548—d23

Manufactured in the United States of America
CPSIA Compliance Information: Batch WS15PK: For Further Information contact Rosen Publishing, New York, New York at 1-800-237-9932

CONTENTS

CRYSTALS

If you use a magnifying glass to study a bowl of salt, you may notice that many of the pieces are shaped like cubes, with flat sides. What you are seeing is a crystal!

ROCK SOLID

Big or small, common or rare, all crystals are solid structures. Every crystal has sharp, clear edges and corners. Many crystals have a particular number of flat faces, or sides. Snowflakes are crystals that form when droplets of water in clouds freeze. Every snowflake is different, but each has six arms, or points.

ice crystals

COMMON CRYSTALS

Ice crystals are unusual because most of Earth's crystals are made from **minerals**. These are natural substances that make up the rocks of our planet. The mineral crystals in many rocks are so tiny we cannot see them. However, in rocks like granite, minerals are larger. Mineral crystals can only grow large enough to see without a magnifying glass if they have space and time. That is why we often find crystals in caves. These crystals have grown undisturbed for a long time.

amethyst crystal

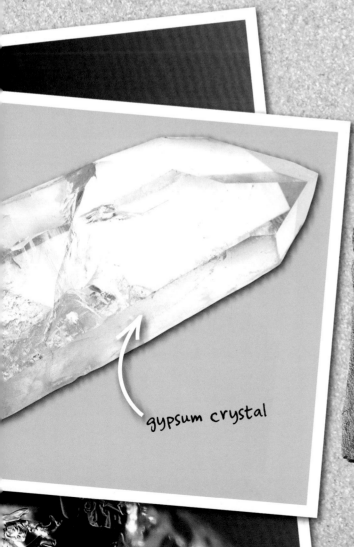

gypsum crystal

ROCK STAR STORIES

In 2008, miners in Mexico were hunting for a useful mineral called gypsum when they found an enormous cave deep underground. Inside they found the largest crystals ever discovered. Some of the crystals were 32 feet (10 m) long and looked like giant white tree trunks! Scientists think the mega-crystals may be half a million years old.

FROM THE DEEP

Deep, deep underground it is far hotter than at Earth's surface, even on a scorching summer's day. It is hot enough for rocks to melt into a mix of minerals called **magma**. Most rock crystals are made from magma.

RISING AND SETTING

Have you watched the blobs of colored wax in a lava lamp? The wax rises as it heats up. That is what happens to hot magma deep underground. Magma rises through existing spaces in underground rock. It also melts new channels through rock. As it rises, magma travels farther from Earth's hot center. Once magma reaches the surface, it is called lava. When it cools down, the minerals in lava **crystallize** to form solid pieces.

lava

GROWING TOGETHER

The building blocks of all crystals, minerals, and anything else on Earth are called **atoms**. Groups of atoms are called **molecules**. In crystals, atoms or molecules are packed together in a very organized way, a little like the way eggs are packed into an egg carton. One carton can sit on another because each egg takes up a particular amount of space. As atoms and molecules from magma are packed together in this organized way, they stack up on top of each other. The molecules and atoms then link together. Over time, these linked rows of molecules and atoms form crystals in rock.

Earth becomes hotter and hotter toward its central core.

Clues to the Past

Diamonds are incredibly tough crystals. They are made of **carbon** atoms that are tightly linked together. Diamonds can only form naturally around 100 miles (160 km) underground where it is very, very hot. The atoms are forced together by the great **pressure** of the magma around them and the rock above them. Diamonds at the surface of Earth all formed deep underground at least one billion years ago. Magma carried them to the surface during **volcanic eruptions**.

diamonds

7

SOLUTIONS

Have you ever watched a rock pool dry up in the sun and wind? Did you notice a dusting of white on the rock, just above the water level? If so, then you witnessed another way in which crystals form: when they grow from **solutions**.

IN A SOLUTION

Nearly all solutions are liquids in which one substance has **dissolved** (mixed with) another substance. Seawater is a solution of salt that has dissolved in water. Many minerals dissolve best in hot water. Water trickles deep underground and heats up as it gets closer to hot magma. It is then better able to dissolve minerals.

CRYSTALS BY MAGIC

Energy in moving air and in the sun's heat also affect water molecules in rock pools. It changes water from a liquid into a gas called **water vapor**. This process is called **evaporation**. When the water changes into a gas, it rises into the air. Only the salt

This salt has crystallized from seawater by evaporation.

molecules that were in the liquid are left behind. The molecules bunch together into larger crystals as the water disappears. The crystals are the white substance you notice on the side of empty rock pools.

Clues to the Past

Some rocks have long **veins** (lines) of crystals such as quartz inside them. These are clues that quartz mineral solutions were once trapped in cracks in the rock. Over time, the water evaporated and the quartz molecules that were left behind formed crystals that filled the remaining space.

quartz vein

ROCK STAR STORIES

making sea salt

In 1866, a miner drilling for oil in rocks near Lake Ontario, Canada, found salt instead! Geologists now know that this Goderich salt deposit covers more than 3 square miles (7.7 sq km), making it the largest salt deposit in the world. It formed when water in an ancient sea evaporated. Over many millions of years, the salt molecules left behind became trapped under many layers of rock.

CAVE CRYSTALS

People who explore underground caves find some of the most amazing crystals on Earth. Caves are natural, dark spaces where crystals can grow undisturbed, and with plenty of space, for many thousands of years.

ROCK-EATING RAIN

Did you know that many caves form because of rainwater? Rainwater dissolves a gas called carbon dioxide. This gas is found in air. When rainwater and carbon dioxide mix, it makes a solution that is as **acidic** as lemon juice. If it touches a soft rock called limestone, the solution dissolves a mineral in the rock called calcite. Little by little, the water eats into cracks in the rocks, dissolving more and more of it, until a cave forms. Then, as more calcite-rich water drips into the cave, amazing crystals form, too.

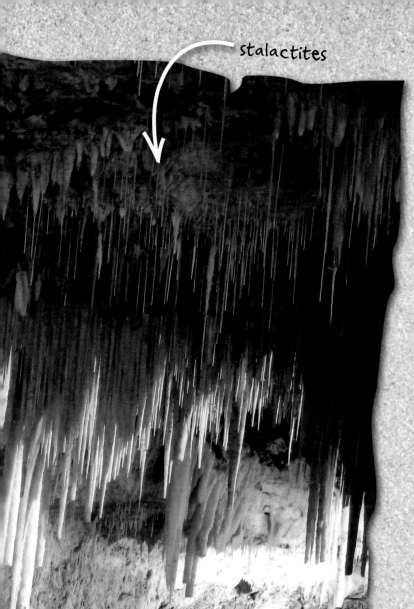

stalactites

CRYSTAL TOWERS

Calcite droplets on the cave roof evaporate, leaving behind tiny calcite crystals. Over time, more calcite builds up around the first crystal. This creates long structures called stalactites, which hang down from the cave ceiling. More and more calcite-rich water drips over the stalactite and down onto the cave floor. Inch by inch, calcite towers called stalagmites grow upward, toward the stalactites.

Clues to the Past

In Mexico, gypsum crystals developed into the largest crystals ever found on Earth. These crystals needed certain conditions to grow. For around half a million years, the limestone caves were filled with a very strong gypsum solution. Nearby magma kept the solution warm, at a constant temperature of 122° F (50° C). In these perfect crystal-growing conditions, more and more gypsum crystallized from the solution, and grew into huge crystals.

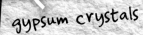

gypsum crystals

CRYSTAL SHAPE

How can we tell crystals apart? After all, there are around 3,000 types of minerals on our planet, and in the right conditions, each can form crystals. One way to spot the difference is by their shape.

SHAPES AND SYMMETRY

All crystals are **symmetrical**. This means that the faces on one side of the crystal are the same shape as those on the opposite side. This is because crystals grow in a regular way. However, different types of crystals have different shapes. They also have different ways of being symmetrical. Salt crystals have four equal square faces. Gypsum crystals also have four faces but they are **parallelograms**. Quartz crystals are a hexagonal shape.

amethyst geode

TRICKY CRYSTALS

Identifying crystals can be tricky because some minerals take on different shapes depending on how they form. Gypsum forms enormous hexagonal crystals in caves, but in dry deserts it forms desert roses. These are pink crystals shaped like roses that grow when gypsum crystallizes around grains of sand in hot conditions. Small crystals of quartz or calcite minerals can grow inward into spaces within rocks called **geodes**.

desert rose

malachite

Clues to the Past

Malachite minerals grow amazing crystals that are shaped like weird, melted bunches of grapes! This shape is a clue to how the crystals formed long ago. In malachite, layers of minerals containing copper form in bands around a speck of sand, dust, or other substance. Over time, many bands of slightly different color build up. Together, they form a sphere shape. Several spheres grow into each other, creating the grapes.

CRYSTAL COLOR AND STRENGTH

Malachite is green, rubies are red, amethyst is purple, and diamonds are colorless. Using these color rules, we can spot many different types of crystals. However, not all crystals follow these color rules!

COLOR CONFUSION

Emerald is a green form of the mineral beryl. However, only some beryl is green. Other types are red, pink, yellow, or blue. Each color is created by different atoms that are trapped within the beryl crystal. Emerald looks green because of the chromium in its crystals. A blue type of beryl is called aquamarine, and it gets its color due to the iron trapped inside the crystal. Fluorite also comes in different colors according to which atoms are trapped inside its crystals.

yellow beryl

red beryl

Shine **ultraviolet (UV) light** on some crystals and they glow with weird and wonderful colors! Pink calcite crystals glow red under UV light. As pink calcite crystals grow, tiny quantities of manganese take up space that calcium atoms would normally take up in the calcite. Rhodochrosite is a mineral that looks identical to pink calcite crystals under normal light. However, it does not glow under UV light, proving it is a different type of crystal.

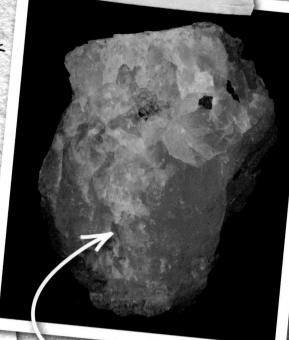

Fluorite crystals glow purple under UV light.

aquamarine beryl

HARD AND HEAVY

Crystals can be confusing because two different types of crystal can look identical, even under UV light. We can tell them apart by testing the hardness of the crystal. Diamond and clear zirconia crystals may look identical, but diamond can easily scratch zirconia because it is harder. Sometimes two crystals look the same and are as hard as each other. Then scientists tell them apart by chipping off a piece of each crystal. The two pieces must be the exact same size. Scientists then weigh the pieces to compare the crystals' **density**.

FINDING EARTH'S CRYSTALS

The solid rock on Earth contains most of the crystals on the planet. However, they are usually hidden out of sight. Rather than break open many rocks in hope of finding crystals, people need to know where to look.

THE RIGHT PLACES

Geologists search for some crystals in certain types of rocks or settings. Many large crystals of rubies and emeralds are found in magma that slowly cools deep underground rather than in magma that rises to the surface and quickly cools. Yellow sulfur crystals are often found around the vents (mouths) of volcanoes because they form from gases that come out of the vents.

Clues to the Past

Diamonds are usually buried within a particular rock called kimberlite. The rock formed long ago from magma that carried the rock from deep underground to the surface.

diamond

ROCK BREAK-UP

Natural processes that are part of the **rock cycle** can reveal crystals at Earth's surface. **Weathering** is when acidic rain, ice, or heat break even the hardest rocks into tiny pieces. **Erosion** is when wind, rivers, and oceans carry the pieces away. This leaves behind the hardest crystals that weather very slowly.

weathered and eroded rock

sulfur crystal collector

ROCK STAR STORIES

Blue flames up to 16 feet (5 m) high shoot from Ijen volcano in Indonesia. The flames appear when sulfur gas, deep within Earth, catches fire. Ijen has some of the biggest sulfur deposits and largest natural blue flames on Earth. People collect and sell the yellow sulfur, which is made into rubber tires and sugar.

MINING CRYSTALS

Miners use different techniques to collect crystals. They usually mine where there are large veins of crystals or deposits of many small crystals. It takes time, money, and effort to mine. It makes sense to mine where there are many crystals.

CRYSTALS FROM ROCK

Miners use powerful drills and diggers to chip away at the rock around a crystal vein. They dig deep underground to reach more of the crystal, so they build networks of tunnels in which to dig. The tunnels are held up by wooden or metal struts to stop them from collapsing. When miners find hard crystals in rock, like diamond in kimberlite, they crush the rock into smaller

Mechanical diggers are sometimes used to dig up crystal-rich rocks.

mine tunnel

and smaller chunks. The diamonds are too hard to be crushed by machines, so only the rock is broken up. Eventually, the rock is crushed into a wet sludge, from which the diamonds can be easily lifted.

CRYSTALS FROM RIVERS

Miners find many crystals, like sapphires, in rivers and streams. The crystals are **deposited** after being eroded from rock elsewhere. Miners scoop up sludge from the riverbed in pans or baskets, then swirl it around to get rid of the mud. When only gravel is left, miners pick out the gems. Some mining companies now use machines to suck up the riverbed sludge and shake away the mud, but people are still needed to spot the valuable crystals.

ROCK STAR STORIES

The biggest diamond mine in the world is Orapa in Botswana, Africa. It is about 0.6 square miles (1 sq km) wide. It sits at the top of two kimberlite columns, which were formed when magma from an ancient volcano cooled. Each year, mining machines dig up and crush around 60 million tons (54 million mt) of rock from Orapa. From this, they recover around 2.4 tons (2.2 mt) of diamonds!

IMPORTANT CRYSTALS

How many crystals do you use in your everyday life? They may include salt and sugar, but did you also know there are crystals in your computers, televisions, and watches? All of these devices and many more rely on crystals.

CRYSTAL SMART

Silicon crystals are an important part of many electronic devices we use every day. Tiny stacks of flat silicon crystals, called **silicon chips**, act like "brains" in many devices. The layers are printed with very tiny patterns. The patterns are a little like road maps and instructions that direct the movement of power between the layers of the silicon chips. Flat silicon crystals are also sandwiched together to make solar cells. These change the energy in sunlight into electricity.

Solar cells make up solar panels.

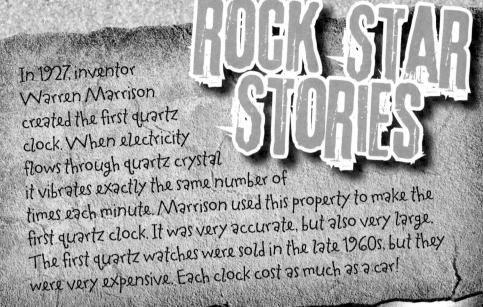

ROCK STAR STORIES

In 1927, inventor Warren Marrison created the first quartz clock. When electricity flows through quartz crystal it vibrates exactly the same number of times each minute. Marrison used this property to make the first quartz clock. It was very accurate, but also very large. The first quartz watches were sold in the late 1960s, but they were very expensive. Each clock cost as much as a car!

Diamond crystals cover the tip of this dental drill.

silicon chip

CUTTING THROUGH

Some crystals are used for cutting materials. The steel cutting edges of drills, like those used by dentists to make holes in teeth or miners to dig wells deep into rock, are tipped with tiny diamonds. They give an excellent cutting surface. Lasers are machines that use crystals to direct powerful beams of light that can cut accurately. Doctors use lasers to carry out delicate eye surgery.

PRECIOUS STONES

Crystals that are especially beautiful and hard to find are very valuable. People buy these expensive gemstones for jewelry and as decorative objects.

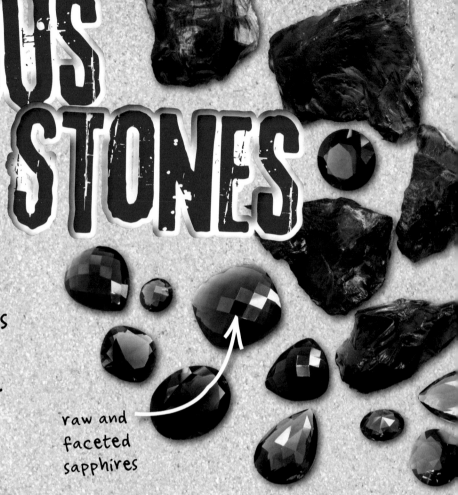

raw and faceted sapphires

PRETTY CRYSTALS

Diamonds, rubies, sapphires, and emeralds are among the most expensive gemstones. People set these gemstones in precious metals, like gold, to make earrings, necklaces, and other jewelry. Gemstone workers also cut crystals into shapes to make sparkling animals and figures that people display in their homes.

SHOWING OFF

The most valuable gemstones are those that are very clear and strongly colored. To make the most of these stones, jewelers

smoky quartz gemstone

use saws to cut a pattern of faces, or flat edges, all over their surfaces. These are called **facets** and they reflect light to make the gemstones sparkle. Jewelers use magnifying glasses while they work to make sure the facets they cut are perfect. After cutting the facets, jewelers also polish crystals to make the flat areas smooth and even shinier.

ROCK STAR STORIES

A plum-sized, perfect pink diamond known as the Pink Star was found in 1999. It is one of the most expensive gemstones in the world. This famous stone was cut and polished for more than two years to reveal its full beauty, and was then mounted onto a ring. In 2013, it sold for $74 million!

Clues to the Past

The ancient Egyptians used crystals for jewelry and decorative objects, too. The kinds of crystals found in Egyptian tombs from more than 3,500 years ago tell us about the people buried there. For example, emeralds, rubies, sapphires, and diamonds were so rare and highly prized in Egyptian times that people who owned them must have either been royals or very important priests.

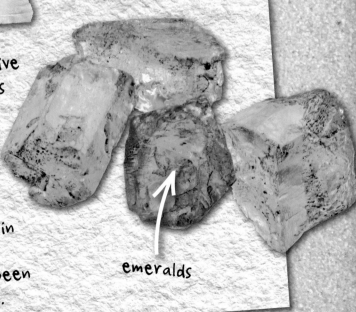

emeralds

23

CRYSTALS ON DEMAND

garnets

Crystals are in high demand in some industries. However, natural crystals of the right size and type may not always be available or may be too expensive to buy. To overcome this problem, people manufacture their own crystals.

GROWING CRYSTALS

Scientists grow some of the large crystals needed to make solar cells, electronics, and lasers. A type of garnet is used to make some lasers. To make the crystal, scientists use a powder containing particular **elements**. They melt it at high temperatures to turn the powder into a liquid. Then a machine holds a tiny crystal of the same mineral, called the **seed crystal**, at the surface of the liquid. Layers of crystal start to form around the seed. The machine turns the seed and very, very slowly lifts it up. Over time, a long cylinder of crystal forms around the seed.

ROCK STAR STORIES

Silicon ingots (blocks) are amongst the biggest man-made crystals. These pure silicon giants are cylinders 12 inches (30 cm) wide and more than 6 feet (2 m) long. In factories, the ingots are carefully sliced into very thin wafers. These are made into solar cells or silicon chips. In the future, people hope to be able to grow even larger ingots to make more useful devices.

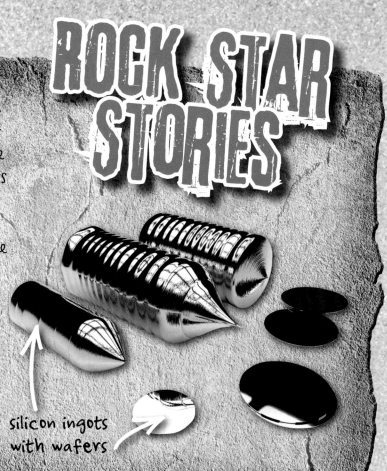

silicon ingots with wafers

UNDER PRESSURE

Scientists make some types of crystals, like artificial diamonds, by recreating the very high pressures and temperatures at which they would form naturally deep underground. They put tiny diamond seed crystals inside special presses that weigh hundreds of tons. Machines squirt a very hot graphite inside the press. Like diamonds, the graphite is made from carbon atoms. The carbon builds up layers around the diamond, making the jewel bigger and bigger.

artificially cut diamond

CRYSTALS IN CRISIS

Crystals are incredible structures that are an essential part of our planet. They are also important resources for use in industry. However, many of the crystals we mine today formed millions of years ago, and very few of some of these crystals are now left. For example, tanzanite is 1,000 times rarer than diamond, and is found only near Mt. Kilimanjaro in Tanzania, Africa.

THE TROUBLE WITH MINING

People need to mine to find certain minerals, but mining is causing damage to the environment worldwide. In some areas, people clear rain forest containing rare animals and plants so they can dig underground in search of crystals. The rock sludge in which miners search for crystals can wash into rivers, and spoil or block them. When miners suck up riverbed gravel in search of sapphires, they destroy fish eggs and many tiny river animals.

The lands around Mt. Kilimanjaro are important for wildlife.

The majority of the world's beaches and deserts are covered with tiny quartz crystals, which form sand. These mini-crystals are the remains of tough rocks, like granite. Most of the minerals that made up the rocks have weathered and eroded away, leaving behind only their light quartz crystals. These are then deposited on land, creating beaches and deserts.

sandy beach

ROCK STAR STORIES

Did you know that crystals are sometimes produced in unethical ways? In some places, crystal miners and gemstone cutters are not paid fairly for their hard work. They also work in dangerous conditions. Sometimes, crystals are mined and sold in order to buy weapons for wars. However, some gem traders are working with the Fair Trade Foundation to make sure that crystal workers have better lives, care for the environment, and do not let crystals get into the wrong hands.

gemstone worker

ROCK YOUR WORLD!

Finding crystals is not always easy, so why not grow some amazing crystals of your own?

YOU WILL NEED:

- white wool
- scissors
- two clean, empty jam jars
- small shallow bowl
- two paperclips
- measuring jug
- hot water from the faucet
- teaspoon
- baking soda
- food coloring

COMPLETE THESE STEPS:

1. Cut a piece of wool about 3 feet (1 m) long. Fold it in half and then in half again. Now twist it tightly.

2. Put the two empty jars on either side of the shallow bowl. Then put a paperclip on each end of the length of twisted wool.

3. Put one end of the twisted wool (and its paperclip) into one jam jar and the other end of the twisted wool into the second jar. (The paperclips help hold the wool in the jars.) The wool should curve slightly above the shallow bowl in between the jars. If it does not, adjust the position of the jars until it does.

twisted wool

4. Add 1 pint (500 ml) of hot water to the jug. Then stir in spoonfuls of the baking soda until no more will dissolve.

5. Add about 15 drops of food coloring to the jug and stir. Then pour enough of this mixture into each jar to cover the ends of the wool.

6. Leave this in a dry, warm place for several days. If a pool of liquid drops into the bowl, empty it back into the jars.

WHAT HAPPENED?

You should be able to see the colored mixture soaking up into the wool. After about two days, small crystals of baking soda should start to form on the wool. Be patient: after about one week, stalactites should start to grow down from the wool too!

TRY IT OUT!

Take an artifical flower with a paper-wrapped stem and dip it into a jar of borax solution. Ask an adult to help you make the borax solution using borax crystals and hot water. Add some food coloring. See what happens to the petals over the week!

GLOSSARY

acidic When a substance contains chemicals that can readily cause changes in others.

atoms Smallest particles of chemical matter that can exist.

carbon Simple chemical substance.

crystallize Form solid crystals from liquid minerals and other substances.

density Measure of the weight of a standard sized piece of a substance.

deposited Put or set down.

dissolved Completely mixed with a liquid.

elements Simplest chemical substances, like iron or carbon.

erosion When soil and rock are carried away by water or wind.

evaporation The change from a liquid into a gas.

facets Flat sides of a gemstone.

geodes Spaces in rocks lined with crystals.

magma Molten rock usually found beneath Earth's crust.

minerals Solid, naturally occurring substances that make up rocks, soil, and many other materials.

molecules Groups of atoms held together.

parallelograms Flat shapes with opposite sides parallel (same distance apart all the way along) and equal in length.

pressure Pushing force.

rock cycle The constant formation, destruction, and recycling of rocks through Earth's crust.

seed crystal A small piece of crystal from which a large crystal of the same material can grow.

silicon chips Tiny pieces of electronic equipment.

solutions Liquids and the substances dissolved in them.

symmetrical Having sides or halves that are the same.

ultraviolet (UV) light Rays of light that cannot be seen.

veins Narrow sections of minerals filling gaps in surrounding rocks.

volcanic eruptions When volcanoes send out rocks, ash, and lava in explosions.

water vapor Water in the form of gas in the air.

weathering When rock is broken down into small pieces by natural processes.

FURTHER READING

BOOKS

Green, Dan. *Scholastic Discover More: Rocks and Minerals*. New York, NY: Scholastic Reference, 2013.

Symes, R.F. *Crystal & Gem* (Eyewitness Guide). New York, NY: Dorling Kindersley, 2014.

Tomecek, Steve. *National Geographic Kids: Everything Rocks and Minerals*. Washington, D.C.: National Geographic Children's Books, 2011.

Walker, Sally M. *Researching Rocks* (Searchlight Books: Do You Dig Earth Science?). Minneapolis, MN: Lerner Publications, 2013.

WEBSITES

Due to the changing nature of Internet links, PowerKids Press has developed an online list of websites related to the subject of this book. This site is updated regularly. Please use this link to access the list: www.powerkidslinks.com/erp/crystals

INDEX

ON THE 5th of Febr. 1857 I left San Francisco with the intention of visiting the ancient Catholic missions which form a cordon from San Francisco to San Diego, comprising all the fertile valleys of the southern counties not distant from the seashore. The first mission and nearest to San Francisco is the Mission of San Francisco, now called "Dolores," which is connected with the above city by a plank road, constructed by a company which levies toll. This road would have been almost impassible to vehicles on account of the deep sand. Of the mission buildings remain only the Church and a building connected with it built of adobe or sunburnt bricks. The building was formerly inhabited by the missionaries but is converted into public houses where the inhabitants of San Francisco are in the habit of resorting.

Leaving the Mission Dolores I pursued the San Jose road to Redwood City, 31 miles distant from San Francisco. This road winds through a beautiful grass country, well adapted for raising stock; the grass had just commenced to sprout and hills and valleys were covered with a green carpet as it were. I arrived at Redwood City by sunset and remained there till morning. Redwood City is a little town of about 50 houses, the inhabitants of which maintain themselves by agriculture and the transit of the "red wood," which belongs to the pine family, which grows to a great height and is cut in the neighboring mountains.

I arrived at Santa Clara in the afternoon. This is a thriving little town situated in the middle of fertile land which is very well watered. Of the ancient Mission, only the Church and a building connected with it remain. The Jesuits have established a college for boys here,

M. and College of Santa Clara.

Misión Santa Clara de Asís
founded Jan. 12, 1777

who are instructed in all the different branches of education. The new college building is a handsome structure and a chapel in the Gothic style is in course of erection. About 150 boys are educated and boarded here by a society of 24 Jesuits with a president at their head.

I travelled from here to the town of San Jose, which is about 2 miles distant from Santa Clara, under the shadow of large poplar and willow trees which were planted many years ago by the missionaries, rendering this road, which is called the Alameda, a pleasant resort of the Santa Clara and San Jose inhabitants.

San Jose is an old Spanish town, now principally inhabited by Americans, who had rendered it one of the most desirable locations in the farming line of California. Gardens and fruit trees spring up everywhere; many streets are planted with rows of ornamental trees. The soil of the large San Jose valley, in which the town is situated, is extremely fertile, and farms are scattered everywhere around. San Jose was once the capital of California and is situated about 7 miles from the Bay of San Francisco in Santa Clara County.

From here I went to the Mission of San Jose, which is about 15 miles from the town of San Jose on the north side of the Bay of San Francisco. The priest, a youth of about 18 years of age, very politely showed me round the ruins which are remaining of this once flourishing Mission. The old adobe Church is a large building, poorly decorated, and surrounded by ruins of a once massive edifice. This Mission is situated in a small valley surrounded by mountains, which are covered in the summer with grass and wild oats.

I went from here to the town of Alviso, the embarcadero at the head of the San Francisco Bay. It is about 6 miles from Santa Clara.

Alviso

M. of San José

Misión San José
founded June 11, 1797

M. of San Juan Bautista

Misión San Juan Bautista
founded June 24, 1797

This place, a kind of a depot of some San Francisco merchants who have warehouses here, favouring the trade between San Jose and San Francisco. This is a horrible mudhole, especially in the rainy season when the streets are almost impassible.

I arrived at Santa Clara, returning from Alviso with the intention to go to the southern missions the 15th of May. We were surprised this morning at about 5 o'clock by a severe shock of an earthquake. This is, however, nothing uncommon in these regions.

On the 9th of May I left Santa Clara pursuing the road toward San Juan Bautista. I travelled through a flat country over a dusty road almost devoid of trees. There was but very little grass for some distance owing to the lack of rain. I met large droves of cattle coming from the southern counties. Afterwards the county had a better appearance and I saw thousands of horses and cattle grazing in all directions. After having travelled about 30 miles, I arrived toward evening to the bed of a dry creek lined on both sides with sycamore trees. According to habit I resolved to camp here, finding plenty of grass for my mule. I built a fire on which I boiled my coffee, having found a little pool of water. I put the fire out, however, before it became dark, to avoid being noticed.

After a few miles riding through a fine and somewhat hilly country I arrived at the San Juan River, which I forded and arrived at San Juan Mission at 10 o'clock A.M., where I dismounted at the Sebastopol Hotel. I proceeded at once to take a sketch of the old mission buildings and town, the greatest part of which are in ruins, and the other part following the same way. The ancient Church is still standing, connected with a long sombre looking building, in front of which is a porch formed by low clumsy arches. Windows are scarce

Misión San Juan Bautista

andrew
Mn of San Juan Bautista

M. of Santa Cruz

Misión Santa Cruz
founded Aug. 28, 1791

Misión Santa Cruz

and small, well provided with iron bars according to the Spanish style. I saw two priests here, one of whom is very old. The Mission and town are located on a high tableland, the descent from which is immediately near the Church and leads into a fine orchard claimed by an American.

Having made a couple of India ink sketches for the proprietor of the hotel, which detained me until the 15th of June, I left on that day for Santa Cruz. The wind is blustering and the dust flies in thick clouds, which rendered my sojourn here very disagreeable to me. Leaving San Juan rather at a late hour, I made my mind up to sleep among the hills but was determined to ride on till I would find water, which I was fortunate enough to find when the sun was nearly setting. 'Twas a small lake, surrounded with plenty of grass for my mule. Having been informed that now and then a stray bear is met in these parts, I kept a look out and slept little. The night was cold and I had to cover myself with whatever covering I could muster and was glad when I saw the morning star and, soon afterwards, the eastern horizon becoming clear. Having taken my coffee, I saddled up and left.

After having passed over some hills, I descended into a large plain covered with grass and over which are scattered numerous farms and many thousands of sheep. After riding a few miles, I had to ford a small river called the Pajaro, on the bank of which is the little town of Watsonville, consisting of but a few houses; many were, however, in course of erection, and I was informed that this place would probably become of importance. My road lead through extensive wheat and barley fields in a flourishing condition. Having rode for some distance over a very level country, I arrived at a very hilly one and

Monterey
founded Dec. 15, 1602

many miles I travelled through a narrow valley (canada). I arrived at Santa Cruz after passing the Santa Cruz River, near the town, and dismounted at the Santa Cruz Hotel.

The Mission and town of Santa Cruz, which is the county seat of the county of the same name, is situated on the northern side of the Bay of Monterey, on the termination of a most fertile valley near the seashore. There is an upper and a lower town. The present upper town, consisting of the ancient Mission Church surrounded by ruins and some houses built in the Spanish style of adobe, covered with tiles, stands on a small flat much higher than the lower town, with which it is connected by a road which runs down very steep. The lower town, being inhabited only by Americans and others coming from the Atlantic states, is constructed in the modern California style, that is of board. Many fine old trees are scattered through the town. In the upper town stands the courthouse and a large hotel together with the mission building and a number of ancient adobe houses, occupied principally by natives, which, however, are unoccupied at present.

A few miles before Monterey I was overtaken by a tremendous rainstorm which wetted me to the skin, being well pleased when I arrived at Monterey, where I dismounted at the Washington Hotel kept by an Italian named Tresconi (21st May).

I rode next day to "Point Pinos" on which is built the lighthouse, 3 miles from Monterey. The keeper of the lighthouse is a woman, whose husband was shot by a notorious bandit named Anastasio Garcia. Being one of the sheriff's posse who went to apprehend said outlaw, and being foremost in entering the house, breaking open the door, he received a pistol ball in his breast, which ended his life in-

Lighthouse near Monterey

Point Pinos

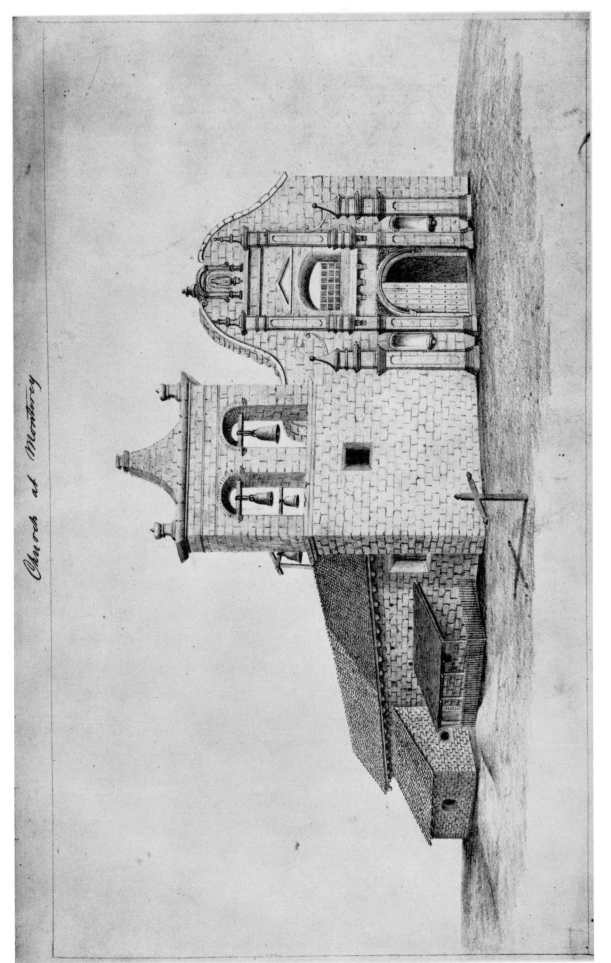

Church at Monterey

San Carlos de Monterey
founded June 3, 1770

Redoute of Monterey

Fort of Monterey

stantly. The assistant keeper invited me to examine the interior of the lighthouse and the light as well as the mechanism and general construction, which is very ingenious and everything kept in the nicest order.

I went to the Carmel Valley, near the seashore at the mouth of the Carmel River where stands what remains of the Mission San Carlos. With exception of a few adobe houses, the whole is a heap of ruins. The old Church, which must have been a handsome one, is partly fallen in; however, the front with two strong belfreys over it is in good condition. There are still remaining two cracked bells, which are said to contain a considerable quantity of silver composition, as most of the ancient Spanish bells have. The inside of the Church has some fresco painting and inscriptions from the Bible. Some saints, as large as life, cut in wood and painted, are still to be seen; they are riddled with bullets, having served as a target. The Mission buildings form a large square. After I had taken a sketch of the place I returned to Monterey.

I took a sketch of fort, or rather, Redout of Monterey, which is located on an eminence commanding the Bay. Captain Baldwin of the Ordnance Department is stationed here with a few soldiers. The few guns and mortars, together with powder and balls and other stores, have lately been removed to Benicia.

Monterey was the capital of the State when the Americans took possession and is built in the Spanish style of adobe, counting about 2,000 inhabitants. It is situated on the southwest side of the Bay of Monterey in a cove. In the background rise high hills which are covered with tall pines.

I left (24th June) Monterey with intention to travel to the Mission of Nuestra Senora de la Soledad, which is distant 45 miles.

M. of San Carlos.

Misión San Carlos Borroméo
founded June 3, 1770

M. of la Soledad

Misión Nuestra Señora Dolorosísima de la Soledad
founded Oct. 9, 1791

There are oaks scattered over the plain which afford a singular appearance, having branches only on one side, having grown by the continual wind into that shape. I met several ranchos, which however had been abandoned on account of the drouth. Not having left early enough to be enabled to make the journey to La Soledad in one day, I struck across the plain towards the mountain chain when the sun was not far from setting, in hope to find some grass for my mule, in which however I was deceived and had to tie the poor animal for a night without food. I arrived at La Soledad at 10 . This Mission is a great heap of ruins with exception of one building and a small church of a modern date. The land of this Mission is owned principally by the numerous native family of the Soberanes. A French Swiss kept a little grocery shop and restaurant here, where I took some miserable coffee and bought some crackers. There being nothing to attract me, I took a quick sketch of these ruins while my mule fed on some straw, which was all that I could procure.

Although there is hardly anything else but ruins left, this Mission was once in a very flourishing condition. The plain in which it is situated is called the "Llano del Rey," and the priests caused the Indians to make an aqueduct of 15 miles length with which they could irrigate over 20,000 acres of land, providing thus against the summer drought.

The sun sinking down fast behind the mountains, I prepared for encampment and tied my mule out in a fine grass plot and laid my blankets down under a dark oak tree. Having been told that bears abound in this canada, I slept very little during the night; was however not molested and saddled up early in the morning, continuing my route towards San Antonio.

I saw in a distance something resembling a cabin and, not fancying to sleep out in this dangerous bear country, I rode towards it, congratulating myself on my good fortune. However, I found, after getting near, that it was a bear trap constructed of heavy logs, closing with a trap door. The massive trap door was kept open by a piece of wood which was placed under it so as to prevent it falling, the trap not being set. For want of a better house, I concluded to make up my bed in the trap, collecting a considerable quantity of dry wood with which I made a fire. After I had made sure the door could not fall down, in which case I would have been caught without the possibility of getting out again, I laid down to sleep. Suddenly I was awakened by a loud report. I looked round and saw that what I had taken great pains to prevent had happened—the trap door had fallen and I was a prisoner. In my sleep I had probably pushed the prop under the door with my foot; it had fallen. I exerted all my power to raise the door but to no avail. I was in a plight. It was past 2 when I heard a yell not far from me and, suddenly emerging from behind a hill, two horsemen, pursuing some cattle, took their direction towards me. I hollered as loud as I could and soon attracted those men's notice, who after having come near and seeing me were lost in wonderment. I related my misfortune to them at which they heartily laughed, working at the same time with a good will to get me out of this dilemma. I found my mule was all right, and, after giving my thanks to my deliverers in a pecuniary manner, they showed me the trail to San Antonio, from which place I was but a few miles distant, where I soon after arrived, and which I found to have preserved a quite better condition than La Soledad. I had much conversation with the jolly priest, who was very talkative and told me many things

M. of San Antonio de Padua.

Misión San Antonio de Padua
founded July 14, 1771

about the former state of the missions, when they were in their flower and after their secularization. He, of course, eulogised the conduct of the missionaries and ran down to zero the public administrators who took the place of the priests. He related to me with what rapacity those men appropriated everything to themselves on what they could lay hands, and what vandalism was perpetrated by one of them who, to save the trouble to send a few miles distant for bark for tanning purposes, had stripped the bark of all the fine pear trees in the orchard.

After having passed a pleasant night, I left in the morning after breakfast for the Mission of San Miguel which is 16 leagues distant. After a ride of about 8 miles, leaving the river to my right, I arrived at a ranch called "Los Possitos" (The Springs) on account of a number of springs which bubble up here and which are as clear as crystal. This rancho is owned by one of the Soberanes, a native Californian. I met several large droves of cattle and horses from San Luis Obispo.

With my pocket compass, I succeeded to find the road, which led me to the River Nacimiento, which at present is not running but forms pools of fine clear water in its sandy bed, round which I observed tracks of various game, but the most plentiful were those of bears and quite fresh.

After watering my mule I rode away from the road, having the habit of never camping near a road, with the object of selecting a green spot for my mule, when getting to a clump of dark trees, a horrible spectacle met my eye. I saw part of an human skeleton bound to a tree; part of the bones had fallen to the ground, the flesh had all gone and only some dried skin was remaining. The skull laid on the ground, cleft in two towards the left temple.

M. of San Miguel.

Misión San Miguel Arcángel
founded July 25, 1797

The vicinity of this river has a notoriety for murders which have been committed here. Only two months ago two drovers were murdered here. I proceeded on my way to Mission San Miguel, where I arrived in 2 hours.

The Mission of San Miguel forms a large square, on which a great number of adobe houses remain, which, however, with exception of the Church and a few buildings next to it, are all unroofed and partly in ruins. The land formerly belonging to the Mission, of which some is very fertile, was of great extent to the amount of 50 or 60 leagues. There are no more Indians, except a few in the employ of Mr. Del Rios, the present proprietor. The above gentleman showed me the interior of the Church, which varies in nothing from all the other mission churches, being a long but narrow building, with whitewashed walls daubed with some coarse fresco painting, an altar stripped of its silver plate, which are replaced with tin. I met eight horsemen here, en route to the Tulare Valley to hunt wild horses.

After having taken a sketch of this Mission, I left towards the Mission San Luis Obispo which is 14 leagues from here. Having left at 3 o'clock P.M. I did not expect to travel far that day (28th of June). My road led alongside of the San Miguel River, with a wide sandy bed, but without a drop of water.

The grass of the country over which I travelled today had all burned off, some incautious travellers having left fire behind which, being blown by the wind, had run on for a number of miles. Finding a pool of fine clear water I camped here for the night. In the morning early I arrived at a rancho, built of adobe, called El Paso De Robles, which was inhabited by some hunters. I found deer to be very plentiful in the vicinity. After crossing a small river near the rancho, I

M. of San Luis Obispo

Misión San Luís Obispo de Tolosa
founded Sept. 1, 1772

struck into a dry and barren tract of 10 or 12 miles, after which the country improved; hills and valleys were covered with wild oats and timber and offered a most refreshing aspect, till I arrived in the vicinity of the Santa Margarita Rancho, where I found the road strewn with petrified shells. I ascertained that the ground over which I rode and the hills to both sides of it, is composed of those seashells, some of which are of large size. A large and well preserved one, I picked up from amongst thousands, which weighed about 15 pounds.

Santa Margarita is located in a very fertile valley, well watered, and served formerly as a storehouse of the missionaries of San Luis Obispo. This house is about 200 feet long with an adobe wall round it. There are a few houses of adobe scattered round, amongst which I observed still those petrified shells, which the natives burn and use for mortar and white wash. Leaving Santa Margarita, I descended a very picturesque canada, full of oak, pine and other trees on which were climbing wild grapevines.

Early in the morning I arrived at the Mission, which is metamorphosed into a little town at present of about 150 houses, inhabited principally by natives and Mexicans; however quite a number of Americans have also settled here. I dismounted at the only hotel in the place, which is kept by two Alsacians near the ancient Mission Church. After breakfast I took a ramble about the mission buildings, some of which are in ruins, though once remarkably strong, constructed of rock joined with a very hard cement. In the building adjoining the Church is held court at present, in the absence of a better one. In one part of this large edifice Fremont was quartered with his riflemen. This is the seat of the County of San Luis Obispo. I was informed by a young and very intelligent American that the Ameri-

San Luis Obispo

Misión San Luis Obispo de Tolosa

can government was very badly sustained here and a jury could not be found to convict a criminal. Of the once magnificent orchards are only a great number of olive trees remaining. There is a sun dial, placed on a stone pillar in front of the mission building, which was placed there by some of the padres.

I left here on the 1st of July, travelling for some miles through immense fields of wild mustard over a level country, after which the road led into a canada, with high hills on both sides, covered with timber. After arriving on the top of a hill, I suddenly saw the sea before me only a few miles distant. While travelling along toward the Mission of Santa Inez, I lost my road by taking the wrong one of the two before me, arriving at a good looking house in the California style. I was directed towards a rancho, called Mapomo, owned by an American, an old settler named Captain Branch who has a sawmill erected here. I was directed here to the right road, which led through a very dense forest famous for robbers. I passed through it however unmolested. After leaving the forest I passed over barren hills for a number of miles, till I arrived at a Californian ranch, where I saw a number of Mexicans. Although the sun was getting low, I resolved to travel on, and, having been informed that I would have to travel six leagues without water, I provided myself with some and left, having made it a point never to pass the night in any of the ranchos on the road on account of their suspicious character. I rode therefore a few miles farther and, finding a green spot where I tied my mule out and which was hid from the road by surrounding hills, I camped.

I rose by daylight in the morning, saddled up and left. The men on the rancho which I passed yesterday did not tell me a story, for I rode a long time without meeting any water. I arrived at last at a

M. of La purísima Concepción

Misión Purísima Concepción
founded Dec. 8, 1787

rancho situated in a beautiful green valley, watered by a small stream. From here I had to ascend some high hills and travelled over a very mountainous country, where I lost my road, which I succeeded in finding again after a tedious search. The mountains in this region are mostly composed of lime rock and white sand, covered with chaparral and grass. Some of the hills which I had to ascend were very steep and very sandy, which was hard on my poor mule. At last I descended into a very extensive flat, at the end of which I perceived some houses. Hoping that this might be the Mission of "La Purissima Conception," in which I was however deceived, for when I arrived at the rancho I found this to be called Santa Rosa, owned by an old widow. All the hills are covered with trails caused by the cattle and may be mistaken for the right road. Having travelled about 4 leagues over a level country, bordered to the right and left by mountain chains, I arrived at the Mission "La Purissima Conception," which is built between some sand hills on one side of a large green valley partly covered with timber. The mission buildings are completely hid to the traveller till coming very near it and by turning round a hill. All the mission buildings, with the exception of one, are in ruins. In this resides the proprietor, named Dr. Juan Malo, a Chilian, with his family. The Church is at the end of the same building. The proprietor was not at home, but his wife, a Californian lady, and some children were present. She was a pleasant little woman, and while I was conversing with her, the cook announced dinner ready, which she immediately invited me to partake, nor would listen to any refusal.

The remaining building is remarkably strong and one of the best preserved ones which I met throughout California. There is still an orchard, a small vineyard remaining. The lady informed me that she

M. Hand College of Santa Ines.

Misión Santa Inés
founded Sept. 17, 1804

owned about 1,000 head of cattle.

This Mission is situated about 18 leguas south of San Luis Obispo, and on the thirteen hundred square miles which was claimed by this Mission was at one time such an abundance of cattle that it was allowed to any to kill the same for their hide and tallow; the meat was left to the wolves and buzzards.

After I had taken my sketch of this Mission I returned to Santa Rosa, near which rancho I camped for the night.

I left early in the morning en route to the Mission "Santa Ynez" which is distant from the Mission "La Purissima" about 7 leguas in a southerly direction. Passing through a hilly country, well timbered, with the river to my right, I arrived at that Mission. It is built on the edge of a table land. The Church, which has a belfry with two bells in it, is in a good condition together with the adjoining house; the rest is a great heap of ruins. The walls of some of the buildings are of an enormous thickness, built of adobe. There is a school established here, called a college, with the priest, an Old Spaniard, presiding. I had some conversation with him and with the schoolmaster, an old Irishman, who was dressed in ragged clothes, horribly dirty. I counted 9 or 10 boys as dirty and ragged as their preceptor, who are most part children of families residing in Santa Barbara.

After having taken a sketch, which was not a pleasant task, being all the time exposed to a burning sun, I left, taking the road towards Santa Barbara, which is 12 leguas distant from this place. After a few miles riding, I arrived at a two-story building in the ancient style, owned by a Frenchman, who is an old settler, being married to a native lady. I accepted his invitation of taking some coffee, which the family was just drinking. During a conversation which I had with him, he informed me that he had the intention to sell his rancho and cattle and leave the country, for the taxes imposed upon his property were ruining him. I heard many such complaints throughout this section of the State. Having crossed the Santa Ynez River, and, having to pass over the mountain chain of about 3 leguas width, I resolved to ride on only for a few miles and camp for the night, with the intention of recruiting the strength of my poor mule and to enable the same to bear the fatigue of ascending the steep trails which I would have to pass the next day. I entered accordingly a canada, well timbered with fine oak and pine trees, and full of wild oats which grew to a considerable heighth.

Next morning I saddled up early and commenced the ascent, still continuing the canada for some time, through which a clear and cold mountain stream was descending. By degrees the canada became more narrow, the mountains higher, and the shadow of the trees darker; in fact the very identical place which a cutthroat might select for his experiments. Steeper and steeper became the ascent, so as to be often compelled to ride up in a zigzag. I often dismounted to let my poor mule rest which was covered with perspiration as well as myself. When I at last arrived at the summit, which could not have been less than 4,000 to 5,000 feet above the level of the sea, I enjoyed a beautiful view over the county and the ocean.

The descent was almost as bad as the ascent, going over fragments of rocks and slippery ravines. There was also a small stream descending which I had to cross repeatedly, by which occasion I discovered a sulphur spring, of a milkish appearance and very nauseous to the taste and smell. I arrived at last at the foot of the mountains at the rancho called Refugio, which is near the seashore, near which the road continued to run over broken and uneven ground, crossed by many small mountain streams.

After a few hours ride I arrived at the Mission Santa Barbara, which lies about one-half mile to the left of the road and two miles from the town of the same name. I resolved to take a sketch of this Mission before going to the town, which I accordingly did. I found here a fine orchard with many pear trees, loaded with ripe pears, of which I bought some of an Italian who seemed to be the proprietor. Judging from the remaining buildings and ruins, this Mission must have been a very flourishing one. A church with two belfreys and the adjoining house, in which the officiating priests live, are in a good state of preservation and built of well cemented rock. A bathing house, large basin and aqueduct rest on arches of the same material.

Being Sunday (July 6th), people from the town and ranchos were coming and going, and masses being said by the priests all day long, I refrained from examining the interior of the church. After having finished my sketch I left for the town, where I arrived about sundown and dismounted at the City Hotel, kept by a Frenchman.

Next morning I ascended a high hill west from the town from which I had a fair view of all the country around, including the Mission, and took a sketch of it. The steamer which plies between San Francisco and San Diego touches here; it had just arrived.

Santa Barbara brings to my memory the old Spanish built towns of Mexico, of which it is an exact counterpart, all houses with a very few exceptions being built of adobe and some of which are really fine two-story buildings, the residences of a number of rich natives, who own the surrounding lands with large numbers of cattle and horses on them. There are a considerable number of drygoods, grocery, and

M. of Santa Barbara.

Misión Santa Bárbara
founded Dec. 4, 1786

Town of Santa Barbara

Santa Bárbara
founded Apr • 21, 1782

Mr. of San Buenaventura

Misión San Buenaventura
founded March 31, 1782

other stores, all of which are owned by Americans, Italians, French-men and Spaniards. The town has about 2,000 inhabitants. The Bay of Santa Barbara is large but unsafe for shipping. I found, travelling through this county, a number of asphaltum springs, by the natives called "brea."

I left Santa Barbara on the 8th early in the morning, taking the road to the Mission of San Buenaventura, which is 9 leguas distant in a southerly direction, also near the seaboard. About a mile out of town I passed a low place, covered with sea salt, where were a number of Indians gathering the salt. The place communicates with the sea which, when spring tide penetrates, fills up this spot. This communi-cation is afterwards discontinued by the falling of the sea. The sea-water, being evaporated by the warm rays of the sun, leaves this de-posit of salt. I travelled along near the seaboard through a very fertile and well timbered country, studded with many small ranchos, among which are quite a number of American squatters. The road now led so very near the sea that the water washed the feet of my mule, while on the other side towering masses of rock threatened to precipitate itself over me, which seem to be often the case here judging by the general appearance, large masses having fallen but recently. I arrived at last without accident at a spot where I left the sea beach, striking into a fine green county, being well watered, where I saw in a distance the belfrey of the San Buenaventura Mission. Finding plenty of grass, I resolved to pass the night here, which I accordingly did. Having passed the night tolerably well, I left in the morning, pursuing my road towards the Mission, which was but a short distance from my camping place and where I arrived after crossing the San Buenaven-tura River. I found it to be quite a village of about 70 or 80 houses, inhabited principally by natives and Mexicans. The Church is in tolerable good preservation, in which officiates a French priest. The mission orchard is still in a fine condition, planted with several hundred large pear trees, loaded with fruit. Part of the mission lands are claimed by some wealthy rancheros.

I dismounted at a sort of hotel kept by a man of Old Spain, and where quite a number of jovial men congregated, all being natives of Old Spain. I tasted here the first native wine raised on the mission, which, although not clarified, tasted excellent but was very strong. After breakfast I took a sketch of the Mission. I had some conversation with the priest, a tall Frenchman, who had served formerly as a soldier in the French army. In order to recruit my mule I stayed here till next morning, when I left for the Mission San Fernando, 16 leguas from my starting place, passing a considerable distance through a barren country, till I arrived near a river which I crossed, riding again through a barren country devoid of trees, as were the surrounding mountains. Although the sun was nearly setting, I resolved to ride on till I would find water and feed for my mule and, perceiving at a distance of a few leguas a dark line of trees, I hoped to find there that which I was in search of. It became very dark and cloudy and presently it began to rain. Not being able to discern the road, I abandoned the reins to my mule, which took me safely to a ranch near the road called "El Triomfo" and which is owned by a wealthy ranchero family named Reyes. Having requested permission to pass here the night, I was received in the house where the table was spread for supper, of which I partook, though the fare did not suit me, consisting of tainted broiled beef, bread, a little cheese as hard as wood, and tea. After supper we went to bed, stretched on a cowhide.

After I had paid my score in the morning, I saddled up and left, not having been treated very cordially, pursuing my road towards the Mission San Fernando, which I was told to be 8 leguas from here. Having had some milk and bread for my breakfast, I could hardly keep the saddle for drowsiness while I travelled along, which is always the case when I drink milk in the morning; being however a tolerable good horseman, I managed to take many little naps on the back of my animal, which jogged along its steady little pace. The road wended through a canada which led into a very extensive valley, bounded in a great distance by a very high mountain chain. At the rancho, called "Encino" (oak) on account of the many oak trees found here, I was directed towards the San Fernando Mission, leaving here the great road, which leads to Los Angeles City. I had yet 3 leguas to ride before getting to the above named Mission, where I, however, arrived in the afternoon, having suffered greatly of the heat, which caused my head to pain very seriously. Not wishing to pass the night at the Mission, I rode some distance from it, towards the hills, from where I perceived running a small stream of clear water, the bed of which I followed and which led me to a small laguna or pond, where I resolved to pass the night.

In the morning I returned to the Mission, of which there are a number of buildings remaining and some in good order. The Church and the building in which the proprietor (Don Andres Pico) lives, are in good condition, built of adobe and white washed. The proprietor and his family being absent, I went to a Frenchman who attends to one of the large orchards and vineyards, for which he shares the profits of the sales of the fruit, wine and brandy, with the proprietor. I took dinner with the gardener and tasted some of the wine

M. of San Fernando.

Misión San Fernando Rey de España
founded Sept. 8, 1797

grown here, which was excellent. The day being very warm, I refreshed myself by eating all the fruit which came in my way, as pears, figs, and prickly pears (tuna), a fruit growing on a gigantic cactus specie, which fruit is yellow and very wholesome and refreshing. Close by this Mission commences the well known Tejon Pass, a wagon road which leads to Fort Tejon and the Tejon and Tulare valley.

This Mission is a fine property. With a good management, the two beautiful vineyards and orchards alone, in which grow an abundance of grapes, pears, apples, apricots, peaches, figs, pomegranates, oranges, quinces, prickly pears, etc., being surrounded by a high adobe wall, would prove a fortune to the proprietor.

The gardener showed me 6 or 7 ounces of gold dust which he had bought from different Indians, telling me that gold was found on all the surrounding hills on the surface, which being washed, when water was not wanting, yielded well. Long before the discovery of gold at Sutter's Mill on the American Fork, gold was washed here, and one house alone exported $30,000 of it. After having taken a sketch of this Mission I left for Los Angeles, which is about 9 leguas from here. Towards evening, after having traversed a dry level country, I arrived at a small river (Los Angeles River) with the rancho called Cahuenga, near the bank. From here the ground became mountainous again, and the road ran through a canada, in which I selected a good spot, full of wild oats and concealed from the road, for my night quarters. A small spring supplied me with water for my coffee and I passed quite a pleasant night. The morning was very foggy and I rode down through the canada into an open country which spread before me to a very great extent, looking in vain however for the city, from which I was about 3 leguas distant yet, and which is hid

City of Los Angeles.

Nuestra Señora la Reina de Los Angeles

founded Sept. 4, 1781

by some hills. After having traversed an uneven country, the city burst suddenly in sight. I rode into the place, leaving my mule at the first livery stable which I encountered and putting up at the . . . hotel, kept by a Mormon family. Going immediately to Wells & Fargo's Express office, I was very much disappointed in not finding my trunk which I had left at Monterey in the Washington Hotel, the proprietor of which had promised me to send it down by the first steamer. Since my departure from Monterey the steamer had passed there twice coming from San Francisco, but my trunk had not been sent. Being in my travelling clothes, dirty and almost ragged, it was impossible to deliver my letters of introduction which I had to some of the first native families in the place. Having the intention to remain here about a month, I hired a little house, after having been a week in the hotel where I could not draw without being disturbed.

From the top of the hill which overlooks the town and on which is thrown up a redout by the American Forces which took the same from the natives, I had a splendid view of the town and the surrounding vineyards, through which I afterwards took a stroll, finding everything in a high state of cultivation. Vineyards, water and muskmelon fields, full of fruit, orchards of pear, orange, figs and a variety of others abounded, all thoroughly irrigated with plenty of water.

Today (14th July) I took a sketch of the city from the abovementioned hill of which I afterwards made a copy in India ink.

The weather is very warm here in the morning till the sea breeze springs up, which blows hard enough, blowing the dust through the streets in dense clouds.

The bay of San Pedro, by which the communication between Los Angeles and San Francisco is kept up, is situated 25 miles from Los

Angeles (southerly), the steamer, running from San Francisco to San Diego touching here. The merchandise and passengers between those two places are sent by land in wagons and stages. The anchorage in the bay is excellent, but there is no settlement.

I had to pay in the hotel $12 a week and $1 a day for my mule. I lived, however, much more economically when I hired a little house which cost me only $6 a month, while I ate at a restaurant twice a day, making my own coffee and tea over an alcohol lamp. I could paint here without being disturbed by anybody. I made several drawings for myself and some India ink sketches for different persons, amongst which was Don Andres Pico, for whom I made a painting in water colors of his Mission of San Fernando.

There are several hundred vineyards at Los Angeles, great part of which supplies the San Francisco market, together with an abundance of fruit of all description. Great quantities of wine and brandy are manufactured, the trade of which is becoming a very important one. The town counts about 4,000 inhabitants, a great number of which are Americans, Germans and French. One part of the town is chiefly inhabited by Californians and Mexicans.

On the 20th of August I left Los Angeles for the Mission San Gabriel, which is about 8 miles from here and stopped at the small public house of the place. I had my mule shod while I took a sketch of the Mission, which forms at present a little village, the haunt of some notorious cattle thieves; murders are committed here frequently often as the result of the fandangos which are given almost every night, breaking up in a row and a stabbing or shooting affair.

The Mission Church is well preserved, being built in a peculiar style different from the other churches. The other buildings, however, are dilapidated or totally in ruins. Near the buildings are very long hedges of prickly pears, now full of ripe fruit, which have been planted by the missionaries round their vineyards and orchards.

I paid a visit to the farm of the Hon. Benjamin Wilson, senator of the County of Los Angeles, who lives about 2 miles from the mission buildings in a charming spot on a gentle acclivity, where he has a large and commodious brick house. Mr. Wilson is a man of means, owning a large tract of land, well watered, with a beautiful lake almost in front of his house. His fine vineyard, in which are 16,000 vines and of which he expects to harvest 10 lb. of grapes of each vine, is one of the best in this country. He will make about 10,000 gallons of wine this year, having still the produce of the past year in his large cellar, amounting to 8,000 gallons of excellent wine. He has a fine orchard of a variety of fruit trees, of which 300 are peach trees of a fine quality and so loaded with fruit that the branches break if not sustained. Mr. Wilson holds out very favorable conditions to emigrants who might settle on his land. From this spot a most extensive view of the country is enjoyed. The mountains of San Diego over 100 miles distant are clearly seen, as also the 17,000 feet high mountain of San Bernardino. Mr. Wilson engaged me to make some landscapes for him, which detained me here till the 6th of September, when I returned to the Mission, where just two murders had been committed. A young man named Evertson, son of the widow of Col. Evertson, who resides here, quarrelled with an Englishman named Mitchell while gambling. Mitchell threw a rock at the other party when the latter drew his revolver killing Mitchell. He was examined by a justice of the peace and discharged. Also a poor Indian was stabbed mortally today.

M. of San Gabriel

Misión San Gabriel Arcángel
founded Sept. 8, 1771

I left here on the 6th of September with the intention to pay a visit to the Mormons at San Bernardino, which is about 55 miles distant in a south easterly direction, passing through the finest of the mission lands, called by the American inhabitants Lexington, but better known as the "Monte," the notorious Monte, where in the course of two years over thirty murders had been committed. The town or rather village is built of 30 or 40 rough looking clapboard houses, forming one street; many adobe houses of more ancient date however are scattered in all directions, hid by an abundance of beautiful trees and high growing corn. The inhabitants of this place are most part squatters.

Having passed the night without accident, I mounted my mule, taking up my road again. I travelled all day over an extensive valley, the mountains on each side stretching themselves high into the sky, of a craggy appearance, with hardly any timber on them. I passed but two or three ranchos, the dusty road leading through a dry and dreary country full of chaparral and very level, till I arrived about 8 or 10 miles from San Bernardino where the country commences to descend gradually, till I arrived at a small river where commences the valley of the San Bernardino Rancho. Passing the river, on the other side of which I found some houses, I continued my road to the Mormon town, where I arrived after a ride of three miles, and after nightfall. Inquiring for a hotel, I was directed to the house of the bishop, named Crosby, where I found quarters for me and my mule.

Next morning I took a ramble over the town, which is laid out regular. Most of the houses are small, built of adobe and have a neat appearance; to each house is allotted a piece of ground of two acres for cultivation, and in the suburbs five acres. Part of the town is well

San Bernardino
founded May 20, 1810

watered. In order to be enabled to take a sketch of the place I had to mount on the top of a haystack, the proprietor of which, a native of South Carolina, an enthusiastic Mormon, endeavored to make Mormonism appear favorable to me. There are a few good looking houses in the place, especially the one which is owned by Mr. Amasa Lyman, the Apostol, which is fronting the square. From a distance it resembles a Mississippi steamboat. The Mormons have selected a lovely spot for their settlement, having bought this rancho from the Lugo family, residing in Los Angeles, for the sum of $80,000, of which, however, only part is paid, the rest bearing high interest. The San Bernardino valley is about seven miles in length, the width being somewhat less. Part of it is well watered by two streams. The valley is surrounded by high mountains, the east side of which is covered with a pine forest and where several saw mills are operating. While making a sketch of the public square, I noted the absence of curiosity amongst the inhabitants, for, being accustomed to have a crowd round me in towns where I am sketching, nobody came near, though plenty passed close to me. One of their doctrines is said to be "mind your own business." The town is inhabited by about 2,000 souls, most of whom are Mormons, 200 having arrived from Australia but a few days before my arrival.

My business being finished, I prepared to leave, for the road towards the Mission San Luis Rey, which is very little frequented. After a ride of about six miles the San Bernardino Valley terminated, the road leading through a canada or narrow valley, in which I passed an Indian village named San Timoteo. Omitting to inquire about the road which I wished to take, I rode about six miles without encountering a human being, when I saw a man with a wagon who informed me that I was taking the road to Gorgonio, being the opposite direction of the one which I ought to have taken. I had to return therefore to San Timoteo. Here the right road was pointed out to me, which I followed over a mountainous country till evening, when I arrived in a large flat country called the San Jacinto Valley. Finding water and plenty of grass here, I passed the night near a little stream, departing in the morning early, following the same road through a well timbered country full of pasture. After riding about six miles, an Indian village came in sight, and at the first house I dismounted and was informed that this place is called San Jacinto and that I was far from the right road to San Luis Rey. The village had a few small and rude adobe houses, all the rest being composed of branches of trees covered with hides of cattle. The Indian, who spoke Spanish, told me that he is the Alcalde of the place, and that I ought to have taken the right hand road when descending into the valley, which passes the Rancho of the proprietor of part of this valley and whose name is Dⁿ. Juan Estudillo. He offered to guide me to the right road for a consideration, which I accepted. Having invited me into his brush shantee, I saw two very old Indian women, one of which was blind, being both dressed in the most primitive California Indian style, being a short petticoat or rather apron, composed of rabbit skins sewed together and bark of a tree. The Indian accompanied me for three or more miles when he thought his presence to be of no more use, pointing out to me the direction which I had to take, giving me a lengthy description of the road, where it turned to the right, where I had to take the left or keep a straight direction, etc., in his opinion very clearly, undoubtedly. Accidentally, and by the aid of my pocket compass, keeping a south westerly course, I hit the right road, and arrived towards evening near a small stream, where I found a little grass for my mule and where I passed the night, at a gap in the mountains which I had to traverse.

It might have been midnight when I was startled by a snorting and jumping of my mule; a fiery-eyed California lion was staring at me.

Continuing my road in the morning, I had to ascend a steep and difficult trail through a narrow canada. After passing two ranchos, one of which is called Montserrate, I arrived at the Mission San Luis Rey in the afternoon, being built on a tableland overlooking an extensive valley. The mission buildings have a very imposing appearance and are built in the ancient Spanish style. On the well preserved Church are two belfreys of considerable height. The adjoining building forms a large square, to which you arrive by a large door under the porch of the building in front, which is composed of 32 arches, resting on solid square pillars. The building in the interior, forming the large square, is constructed in the same style, with a porch running all round, all the buildings being covered with tiles. In the middle of the square is a mound of earth, with a low wall round it, out of which grows a beautiful black pepper tree, full of fruit, clad in the finest green.

The interior of the Mission is in a very good condition. Near the buildings are a few huts in which live some Indian families. Having been informed that I might find entertainment at the house of an American, named Tibbets, about one-half mile from here, I rode down and finding this to be the case, I dismounted. This man is married to a native woman and raises a quantity of water and muskmelons which were just ripe. Not having any accommodations in his house for strangers, I mounted the haystack in which I slept like a prince.

In the morning I went up to the Mission with the intention of

Misión San Luís Rey de Francia
founded June 13, 1798

taking a sketch and where I found stationed a sergeant and two soldiers—all Irishmen in Uncle Sam's service, who were sent here to guard the mission buildings and what remains in it against robbers and vandalism. After finishing my sketch I returned to Tibbets, where I remained till the following day.

On the 14th of September I left San Luis Rey for San Diego and passed through a very hilly country, part of it full of pasturage, cattle and horses, the road passing but a few miles from the seashore. Repeatedly I met pools of water which, however, was very salt. At 8 o'clock in the evening I arrived at San Diego, where I dismounted at the public house of a Mr. Rose, a German and a man of considerable enterprise, who dabbles in everything. He owns a number of houses, has purchased several thousands of town lots at the most desirable spot at the entrance to the harbor from the sea, with the expectation of making millions if the eastern railroad might terminate here; he has several ranchos, a tannery, and a public house, is boring for bituminous coal and an artesian well, sends out hunters, etc., and seems to be a clever kind of a man who keeps this otherwise dull little town somewhat alive. The Bay of San Diego is, next to the Bay of San Francisco, the best on this coast. The entrance is very narrow, but deep enough for any vessel, having from 5 to 10 fathoms of water. The town of San Diego is built on an elevation about three miles from the beach; right in front near the entrance to the harbor is a high tableland on which is a lighthouse. This town is only three miles from the boundary line and had a considerable trade formerly. It has about 2,500 inhabitants, who seem to get poorer every day.

At some future time San Diego cannot fail to become a place of great importance. Its position near the Mexican frontier and its splen-

Misión San Diego de Alcalá
founded July 16, 1769

did harbor and other advantages justify this prediction.

I took a sketch of the town, after which I went to the Mission, which lies in an easterly direction from here, about six miles distant, on the end of a fine valley full of pasture. This was the first missionary establishment in Alta California and was founded by Father Junipero Serra in 1769. The mission buildings have lost their ancient appearance, having been renovated by the government, and serve now as the quarters of United States troops. There are several buildings erected by the government and a tall flagstaff with the Star Spangled Banner waving from one. Being built on an elevation, it offers a fine view; below it are numerous olive trees, together with some palm and fruit trees.

On the 21st of September I left this town, offering no attractions, well contented to leave behind me the dreary bay, without shipping, and the sluggish natives and Mexicans, living in contented misery. Having the intention to travel back by land to Los Angeles, and from there to take the steamer for San Francisco, I returned on the same road to San Luis Rey, where I arrived the next day and, providing myself only with some pears, I pursued my road towards the Mission San Juan Capistrano, northwards, being the only mission which I had not visited yet, and which is 12 leguas from San Luis Rey north and 18 leguas south from San Gabriel. I had the intention on my outset to take the road to Santa Margarita, Pio Pico's rancho, which had been praised to me on account of its romantic location and beauty, but missed the road. Few miles from the Mission I met a Californian family, the female part of which were seated in an oxcart of as primitive a construction as possible; the males on horses and mules. From the valley in which San Luis is located I had to ascend in a canada to

San Diego

San Diego

founded Nov. 12, 1602

a more hilly country, the road leading near the seashore. I passed through a barren and dreary country with thousands of cattle, marveling on what those animals sustained their lives. Towards evening I arrived at an old adobe building, formerly a storehouse of a mission where I intended to pass the night, hoping to find something to eat for my mule. I was, however, deceived, for there was not a soul to be found and I had to proceed farther, till night overtook me, without finding any grass for my mule, being compelled at last to dismount and pass the night here. With daylight I mounted and after four or five miles riding came to another rancho of Pio Pico, named San Mateo. From there I had to ride along the seabeach, till I arrived at the Mission San Juan Capistrano, the buildings of which are a few miles from the beach in a beautiful green valley which is well watered by a small stream. I slept in the house of a Polish Jew who had a drygoods and grocery store in the Mission; he also keeps a billiard-saloon. The principal feature of this Mission is the ruins of an once magnificent church, built very solid of rock and cement, with arched roofs. More than half of the Church was thrown down in 1812 by an earthquake and buried under its ruins 30 persons. Some of the mission buildings are in good condition, inhabited by the padre, and Mr. John Foster, an Englishman, a son-in-law of Pio Pico. There are besides fifteen or twenty other houses, of which the house of Dⁿ. Juan Avila deserves notice. I saw great numbers of cattle all along the valley. I was glad when day broke for the fleas in the Jew's house nearly carried me off, and I left as soon as manageable. After riding through a very lonely country, passing the rancho of Don Jose Sepulveda, a wealthy Californian, who is said to keep 500 tame and very choice horses, I arrived at the Santa Anna River, where I passed the

M. of San Juan Capistrano

Misión San Juan Capistrano
founded Nov. 1, 1776

night in the cottage of a poor ranchero who lives on the land of D^n. Juan Carrillo. I saw here cornstalks with seven large ears; the fields, not being fenced in, however, are constantly invaded by cattle.

Not being able to get any breakfast here, I left early, crossing the country without minding the roads, taking the direction in which the Rancho del Puente is situated, about five miles from the town of Lexington and twelve miles from Los Angeles, owned by an Englishman of large property. Passing his rancho on my road from San Gabriel to San Bernardino, I had promised to pay him a visit at my return, with the purpose of making some sketches for him. After having crossed a large tract of a level country, I arrived at a rancho called "Coyotes," from where I had to cross a mountain chain till I arrived in the large valley where Mr. Workman lives.

Amongst the drawings which I made for Mr. Workman was a plan for a chapel which he is going to build here to the benefit of his Indians who live near his house in their shantees and who work for him, earning 50c a day. Mr. Workman's house is a one story building of adobe and forms a square with a yard in the middle. The house is well finished, and painted with oil colors on the inside and outside, imitating marble, and afterwards varnished. On the flat roof over the gate is placed a handsome square apartment on which is a little turret, having a very imposing and neat appearance. There is a fine and large vineyard and orchard in which grow 12,000 grape vines and an abundance of fruit of all kind, of which the coyotes are very fond, and for which reason meat poisoned with strychnine is laid in the vineyard, which the coyotes never fail to eat and die. On the 13th of October, having finished my sketches, I returned to Los Angeles, from where I went to San Francisco by the Steamer *Seabird*.

These will enthrall you:

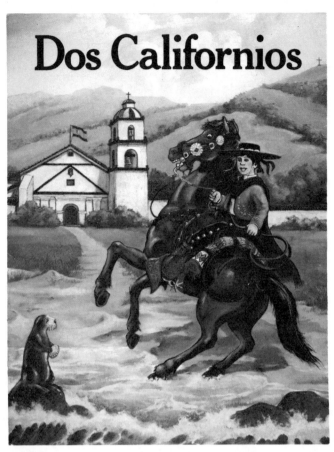

English & Spanish, about boy, sea otter & pirate, $2.95

The story of a girl at the Bear Flag party, 1846. $3.50

We had *very* exciting chiefs here, too. $3.50

In lovely color, exciting history of ancient times, $4.95

Forest
HABITATS

BY ARNOLD RINGSTAD

Published by The Child's World®
1980 Lookout Drive • Mankato, MN 56003-1705
800-599-READ • www.childsworld.com

Acknowledgments
The Child's World®: Mary Berendes, Publishing Director
Red Line Editorial: Editorial direction
The Design Lab: Design
Amnet: Production

Photographs ©: Brand X Pictures, cover, 1; Shutterstock
Images, back cover, 6–7, 10, 23; Eric Isselee/
Shutterstock Images, back cover; Joyce Vincent/
Shutterstock Images, 5; Leonid Ikan/Shutterstock Images,
8–9; SP Photo/Shutterstock Images, 13; Brian Lasenby/
Shutterstock Images, 14–15; Wesley Aston/Shutterstock
Images, 16; Gerald Marella/Shutterstock Images, 19;
Digital Vision, 21

ISBN 9781623239909
LCCN 2013947268

Printed in the United States of America
Mankato, MN
December, 2013
PA02192

Table of Contents

Welcome to the Forest!

Forests are important habitats. Habitats are the places where living things get everything they need. Trees make up the biggest part of forests. Trees are not the only things living in forests. Many other plants and animals live on the ground. Birds fly high above the forest **canopy**.

Ten percent of Canada is covered in forests.

Living things in the forest work together. Trees give shade and food to animals. Animals eat harmful insects to save trees. Tiny creatures live on the forest floor. They become food for larger creatures.

Earth's forests are in danger. One danger is **logging**. Cutting down too many trees can affect all life in the forest. Other dangers include fires and pollution. It is important for humans to take care of forests.

Leaves and branches from forest trees create a forest canopy.

Where Are the World's Forests?

Forests can be found all across the world. They cover about one third of the land on Earth. The United States and Canada have many large forests. Europe, Asia, South America, and Australia also have forests. There are three different kinds of forests.

Deciduous forests are in the eastern United States and Canada. Western Europe also has this type of forest. Deciduous forests are far from the **equator**.

Coniferous forests are in the northwestern United States. They are also in southwestern South America and in Asia in Japan. These forests

Forests are found across the world on every continent.

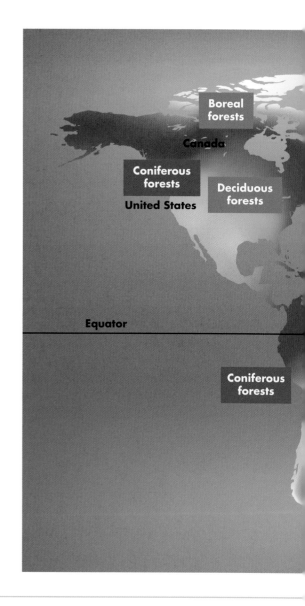

Boreal
forests

Canada

Coniferous
forests

Deciduous
forests

United States

Equator

Coniferous
forests

are farther from the equator than deciduous forests. Coniferous forests can be found near coasts or mountains.

Boreal forests can be found in northern areas. They are farthest from the equator. These forests are in Canada, and in Northern Europe in Denmark, Norway, Sweden, and Finland.

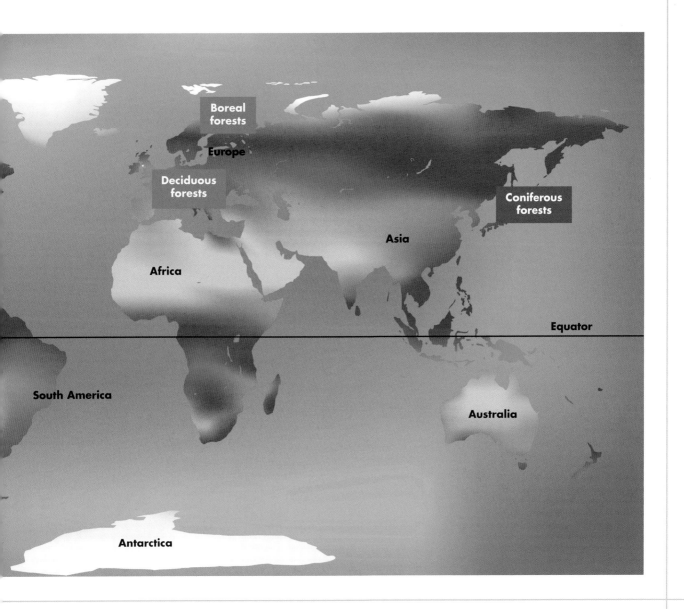

What Do Forests Look Like?

The three types of forests each look different. The weather changes in each area. Different types of trees also grow there.

Deciduous forests have trees that lose their leaves during winter. Their soil is good for growing. The soil is a good mixture of dirt to plant in. Many kinds of plants grow beneath the tall trees.

Trees in coniferous forests do not lose their leaves in winter. They have special leaves called needles. The trees keep their needles year-round. These forests also have good soil for growing.

Coniferous trees keep their needles year-round.

Boreal forests also have trees with needles. But their soil is thin and not good for growing. Few plants grow under the trees in these forests.

Deciduous forests are the only type of forest with four seasons.

Long Winters, Short Winters

Deciduous forests get hot in summer and cold in winter. Rain falls in spring, summer, and fall. Snow falls in winter. These forests get up to 60 inches (150 cm) of rain and snow each year.

The temperatures in coniferous forests stay about the same all year. These forests get more **precipitation** than deciduous forests. They can get up to 200 inches (500 cm) each year. This makes it is easy for trees and other plants to grow.

Boreal forests are cold most of the year. They have long winters and short summers because they are in the North. They get less precipitation than other forests. Usually they get about 40 inches (100 cm) of precipitation each year. Most of this is snow.

Boreal forests receive many inches of snow during the long winters.

The Plants
of the Forest

The biggest plants in forests are trees. There are two main types of trees. The first type is deciduous. The second type is coniferous. Deciduous trees lose their leaves in the winter. Coniferous trees do not.

One important deciduous tree is the maple tree. The maple gives shade to forest animals. Humans also use these trees. Maple syrup for pancakes comes from inside them. Wood from maple trees is used to make furniture.

The pine tree is an important coniferous tree. Birds and squirrels eat its seeds to survive. The seeds of coniferous trees are found in pinecones. Hungry animals take these pinecones. They eat the nut inside the pinecone. This spreads the seeds across the forest and helps more trees grow.

Not all plants in the forest are trees. Many plants live in the **undergrowth**. One of these is moss. Moss grows on the ground, rocks, and trees. Thick moss looks like green carpet. It needs wet and shady places to grow. The tall trees give it shade. The tree roots collect water to help the moss grow.

Pinecones and moss cover much of forest floors.

Living in the Undergrowth

Many kinds of animals live in deciduous and coniferous forests. Tiny bugs and huge mammals live in the trees. They also live among the plants on the ground.

White-tailed deer use the undergrowth to survive. Sometimes mother deer search for food. They leave their babies hidden in the undergrowth. There the baby deer are safe from other animals.

Stick insects look like twigs. They blend into the branches. They can hide from birds that eat them. If a stick insect notices a bird nearby, it stands still. Then it pulls its legs closer to its body. This makes it look even more like a stick.

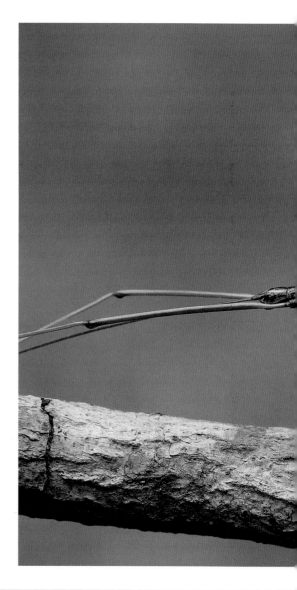

Stick insects are hard to find in forests because they blend into tree branches.

Red foxes also live in these forests. They eat animals and fruit. When they eat fruit, they help carry seeds to new places. This helps the plants spread. Red foxes eat small animals, such as mice. Red foxes can sometimes become food for large animals, such as bears.

Living in the Cold Forests

Animals living in boreal forests are able to survive in the cold. Many have thick fur. The fur keeps them warm when cold winds blow.

Moose have special stomachs to keep them warm. Their stomachs create heat when they eat. Moose cannot sweat. This also keeps them warm. Moose cannot live in hot places over 80 degrees Fahrenheit (27°C).

Salmon live in the rivers of boreal forests. They are born in the rivers and travel to the ocean. They return to the rivers to have babies. Bears eat salmon from the river. They leave some salmon meat behind in the forest. This brings **nutrients** from the ocean to the forest. The nutrients help the forest plants grow.

Snowshoe hares' fur turns brown during the summer. They match the dirt and trees. During the winter, their fur changes to white. White fur helps them match the snow. The color changes help the hares hide from enemies year-round.

Forests are a good place for moose to live because of the cool temperatures.

Woodpeckers of the Forest

One amazing animal of the forest is the woodpecker. Woodpeckers live in all kinds of forests. They live everywhere except Australia and Antarctica.

Most woodpeckers weigh about 1 pound (0.5 kg).

Woodpeckers are famous for the tapping sound they make. This noise happens when they tap their beaks against trees. Woodpeckers can tap 12,000 times each day!

Woodpeckers tap to get food. Each tap digs a deeper hole into a tree. They tap until they find bugs. Then they use their long, sticky tongues to get the bugs out. Some woodpeckers tap to talk to other woodpeckers. Others tap to get the attention of a mate. A mate is an animal to have babies with.

Digging holes in trees is easy for woodpeckers to do with their strong beaks.

Threats to the Forest

There are many different dangers to forests. One problem is **acid rain**. This happens when factories or cars are near the forest. The pollution goes into the clouds. It sometimes falls as acid rain. This rain damages leaves. It also makes it harder for seeds to grow.

Another big problem is road construction. People cut down trees when they build roads through forests. Dead trees do not create oxygen, shade, or food. This logging can kill the plants near these trees. It harms animals that use these plants for food and housing. The animals that carry seeds can disappear. This makes it hard for those plants to spread. People must plant new trees after logging.

Forest fires are also a serious problem. Warmer temperatures can make forests drier. Dry wood makes it easier for fires to start and spread. Forest fires destroy animal habitats. They can also be dangerous to people living nearby. Taking care of the world's forests is important for humans' survival. It is also important for the animal and plant life in forests. Protecting forests is good for the earth.

Logging kills plants and trees in healthy forests.

GLOSSARY

acid rain (ASS-id RAYN) Acid rain has increased acidity from the environment. Acid rain is a danger to forests.

boreal (BOHR-ee-al) Boreal forests are in northern areas of the world. Boreal forests are farthest from the equator.

canopy (KAN-uh-pee) The branches and leaves of treetops form a canopy. The forest canopy gives shade to the ground below.

coniferous (KON-uh-fur-uhss) Coniferous forests have trees with needles and cones. Coniferous forests are near coasts or mountains.

deciduous (di-SIJ-oo-uhss) Deciduous forests have trees with broad leaves. Deciduous forests are far from the equator.

equator (i-KWAY-tur) The equator is an imaginary line running around the middle of Earth from east to west. Deciduous and coniferous forests are far from the equator.

logging (LOG-ing) Logging is cutting down trees. Logging in forests kills animals and plants.

nutrients (NOO-tree-uhnts) Nutrients are needed by living things to stay healthy. Nutrients help the forests grow.

precipitation (pri-sip-i-TAY-shuhn) Precipitation is rain or snow. Some forests receive more precipitation than others.

undergrowth (UHN-dur-grohth) The plants living below the trees in the forest are called undergrowth. Baby deer hide in the undergrowth.

TO LEARN MORE

BOOKS

Burnie, David. *Tree (DK Eyewitness)*. New York: DK, 2005.

Kalman, Bobbie. *A Forest Habitat*. New York: Crabtree, 2007.

King, Zelda. *Examining Forest Habitats (Graphic Organizers: Habitats)*. New York: Rosen, 2009.

WEB SITES

Visit our Web site for links about forest habitats:
childsworld.com/links

Note to Parents, Teachers, and Librarians: We routinely verify our Web links to make sure they are safe and active sites. So encourage your readers to check them out!

INDEX

ABOUT THE AUTHOR

Arnold Ringstad lives in Minnesota. He likes to visit the local zoo so he can see animals from all kinds of habitats.